MW00457021

HYGINUS - FABULAE

HYPLERN – LEARN LATIN WITH BEGINNER STORIES

Interlinear Latin to English

TRANSLATION
DR TH VAN DEN END

NOTES & EDITOR
CAMILO ANDRÉS BONILLA CARVAJAL PHD

Toronto

2018

ISBN: 978-1-988830-67-4

HypLern

LEARNING A FOREIGN LANGUAGE should not be the product of leafing through pages in a bilingual dictionary until hurting one's fingertips. Quite the contrary, everyday language use, friendly reading, and direct exposure to the language should become the path towards the mastery of vocabulary. In this manner, learners could be successful in the foreign language without too much study of grammar paradigms or rules. Indeed, Seneca expresses in his sixth epistle that "Longum iter est per praecepta, breve et efficax per exempla[1]».

The HypLern series constitutes an effort to provide a strongly effective tool for experiential foreign language learning. Those who are really interested in addressing the original literary works to learn a foreign language do not have to use conventional graded texts or adapted versions for novice

---

[1] "The journey is long through precepts, but brief and effective through examples". Seneca, Lucius Annaeus. (1961) *Ad Lucilium Epistulae Morales*, vol. I. London: W. Heinemann.

readers. The former only distort the actual essence in literary works, while the latter are highly reduced in vocabulary and relevant content. This collection aims at facilitating the lively experience for learners to go through stories as directly told by their very authors.

Most excited adult language learners tend to ask their teachers for alternatives to read writers' thoughts *in* the foreign language, rather than reading others' opinions *about* the target language. However, both teachers and learners lack a reading technique or strategy. Oftentimes, students conduct the reading task only equipped with a bilingual dictionary, a schooling grammar and lots of courage. These efforts usually end up with mis-constructed nonsensical sentences as the final product of long hours spent in an aimless translation drill.

Consequently, we have decided to develop this series of interlineal translations intended to afford a comprehensive edition of unabridged texts. These texts are presented as they were originally written with no changes in word choice or order. As a result, we have a translated piece conveying the true meaning under every word from the original work. Our readers receive then two books in just one volume: the original version and its translation.

The reading task becomes something different from a laborious exercise of patiently decoding unclear and seemingly complex paragraphs. In contrast, reading will be an enjoyable and meaningful process of cultural, philosophical and linguistic learning. Independent learners will then be able to acquire expressions and vocabulary while understanding pragmatic and socio-cultural dimensions of the target language by *reading in* it, instead of *reading about* it.

Our proposal, however, does not claim to be a novelty. Interlineal translation is as old as the Spanish tongue, e.g. "glosses of [Saint] Emilianus", interlineal bibles in Old German, and of course James Hamilton's work in the 1800s. About the latter, we remind the readers, that as a revolutionary freethinker he promoted the publication of Greco-Roman classic works and further pieces in diverse languages. His effort, such as ours, sought for lightening the exhausting task of looking words up in large glossaries as an education practice: "if there is any thing which fills reflecting men with melancholy and regret, it is the waste of mortal time, parental money, and puerile happiness, in the present method of pursuing Latin and Greek[2]".

Additionally, John Locke appears as another influential figure in the same line of thought as Hamilton. Locke is the philosopher and translator of the *Fabulae AEsopi* in an interlineal plan too. In 1600, he was already suggesting that interlineal texts, everyday communication and use of the target language could be the most appropriate ways to achieve language learning:

> ...the true and genuine Way, and that which I would propose, not only as the easiest and best, wherein a Child might, without pains or Chiding, get a Language which others are wont to be whipt for at School six or seven Years together...[3].

---

[2] In: Hamilton, James (1829?) *History, principles, practice and results of the Hamiltonian system, with answers to the Edinburgh and Westminster reviews; A lecture delivered at Liverpool; and instructions for the use of the books published on the system.* Londres: W. Aylott and Co., 8, Pater Noster Row. p. 29.

[3] In: Locke, John. (1693) *Some thoughts concerning education.* Londres: A. and J. Churchill. pp. 196-7.

Who can benefit from this edition?

We identify three kinds of readers, namely, those who take this work as a search tool, others who want to learn a language by reading authentic materials, and the last group that attempts to read writers in their original language. The HypLern collection constitutes a very effective instrument for all of them.

➤ For the first target audience, this edition represents a search tool to connect their mother tongue with that of the writer's. Therefore, they have the opportunity to read over an original literary work in an enriching and certain manner.

➤ For the second group, reading every word or idiomatic expression in their actual context of use will yield a strong association among the form, the collocation and context. This very fact will have an impact on long term learning of passive vocabulary, gradually facilitating the reading in their original language. This book stands for an ideal friend not only of independent learners, but also of those who take lessons with a teacher. Simultaneously, the continuous feeling of achievement produced in the process of reading original authors is also a stimulating factor to empower the study[4].

➤   Finally, the third kind of readers may as well have the same benefits as the previous ones. In effect, they definitely count on a unique version from its style. The closeness feature of our interlineal texts is even broader than collections, such as the Loeb Classical Library. Although their works could be the most famous in this genre, their presentation of texts in opposite pages hinders the link between words and their semantic equivalence in our tongue.

---

[4]   Some further ways of using the present work include:
1. As Reading goes on, learners can draw less on the under line (i.e. the English translation). Instead, they could try to read through the upper line with text in the foreign language.
2. Even if you find glosses or explanatory footnotes about the mechanics of the language, you should make your own hypothesis on word formation and syntactical function in a sentence. Feel confident about inferring your language rules and test them progressively. You could also take notes concerning those idiomatic expressions or special language usage that calls your attention for later study.
3.   As soon as you finish each text, check the reading in the original version (with no interlineal or parallel translation). This will fulfil the main goal of this collection: bridging the gap between readers and the original literary works, training them to read directly and independently.

Why interlinears?

Conventionally speaking, tiresome reading in tricky circumstances and through dark exhausting ways has been the common definition of learning by texts. This collection offers a friendly reading format where the language is not a *stumbling block* anymore. Contrastively, our collection presents a language as a vehicle through which readers could attain and understand their authors' written ideas.

While learning to read, most people are urged to use the dictionary and distinguish words in multiple entries. We help readers skip the hard and vague step on uncertainties from grammar paradigms and several meanings. In so doing, readers have the chance to invest energy and time in understanding the text and learning vocabulary; they read quickly and easily as a skilled horseman cantering through a book.

Thereby we stress on the fact that our proposal is not new at all. Others have tried the same before, coming up with evident and substantial outcomes. Certainly, we will not be pioneers in designing interlineal texts, but we are nowadays the only, and doubtless, the best in providing you with interlinear foreign language texts.

HANDLING INSTRUCTIONS

Using this book is very easy. Each text should be read three times at least in order to explore the whole potential of the method. Firstly, the reading is devoted to compare words in the foreign language to those in the mother tongue. This is to say the upper line is contrasted to the lower line as the example shows:

Hanc	materia,	quam	auctor	Aesopus	repperit,
This	*matter*	*which*	*the-author*	*Aesop*	*has-found,*

ego	polivi	versibus	senariis.
I	*have-polished*	*with-verses*	*of-six-feet-each.*

Reading needs to be carried out as follows:

Hanc *this* materiam, *matter* quam *which* auctor *the-author* Aesopus *Aesop* repperit, *has-found* ego *I* polivi *have-polished* versibus *with-verses* senariis *of-six-feet-each* etc...

The second phase of reading focuses on catching the meaning and sense from the English line. Readers should cover the under line with a piece of paper as we illustrate in the next picture. Subsequently, they try to guess the meaning of every word and whole sentences drawing on the translation only if necessary.

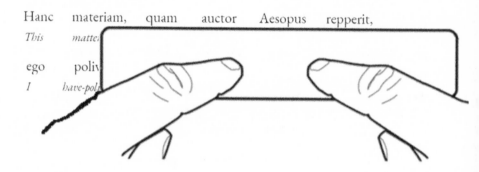

Finally, readers will be able to understand the message in the text when reading it without additional help.

Hanc materiam, quam auctor Aesopus repperit, ego polivi versibus senariis...

Above all, readers will not have to look every word up in a dictionary to read a text in the foreign language. This time they will particularly concentrate on their principal interest. These new readers will tackle authentic texts while learning their vocabulary and expressions to use in further communicative (written or oral) situations. This book is the first work from an overall series with the same purpose. It really helps those who are afraid of having "poor vocabulary" feel unconfident about reading directly in the language. To all of them, welcome to the amazing experience of living a foreign language.

Table of Contents

Chapter I

PANDORA
Pandora

Prometheus	Iapeti	filius	primus	homines	ex	luto
Prometheus	of Iapetus	son	the first	humans	out of	clay

finxit.	Postea	Vulcanus	Iovis	iussu	ex	luto
moulded	Afterwards	Vulcanus	of Iupiter	by order	out of	the loam

mulieris	effigiem	fecit,	cui	Minerva	animam	dedit,
of a woman	the likeness	made	to whom {quis3}	Minerva	a soul	has given gave

ceterique	dii	alius	aliud	donum	dederunt.
and the other	gods	another	something else each a different	gift	have given gave

Ob	id	Pandoram	nominarunt.	Ea	data	in
Because of	that	Pandora	they named (her)	She	(was) given	in

coniugium	Epimetheo	fratri.	Inde	nata	est	Pyrrha,
marriage	to Epimetheus	(her) brother	Therefrom	born	is	Pyrrha

quae	mortalis	dicitur	prima	esse	creata.
which	mortal	is said	the first	to be	created

PROMETHEUS
Prometheus

1

Homines antea ab immortalibus ignem petebant neque
Men — formerly — from — the immortals — the fire — requested — and not

in perpetuum servare sciebant. Postea Prometheus
in / for — ever — to conserve (it) — knew — Afterwards — Prometheus

in ferula detulit in terras, hominibusque
in / inside — a cane — has brought (it) down — in / to — the earth — and to the humans

monstravit quomodo cinere obrutum servarent.
has showed — how — by ash {cinis5} — covered — they (could) conserve (it)

Ob hanc rem Mercurius Iovis iussu deligavit
Because of — that — thing / deed — Mercurius — of Iupiter — by order — has bound up

eum in monte Caucaso ad saxum clavis ferreis.
him — in / on — the mountain {mons5} — Caucasus — at/to — a rock — with nails — iron

Aquilam apposuit, quae cor eius exesset. Quantum
An eagle — he has put there — who — heart — his — should eat out — As much as

die ederat, tantum nocte crescebat. Hanc aquilam
by day — he ate — so much — at night — grew (again) — This — eagle

post xxx annos Hercules interfecit eumque liberavit.
after — thirty — years — Hercules — has killed — and him — has liberated

VULCANUS
Vulcanus

Vulcanus cum resciit Venerem cum Marte clam
Vulcanus — when — he found out — Venus {Venus4} — with — Mars — secretly

concumbere et se virtuti eius obsistere
to lay down — and — he himself — to the strength {virtus3} — his (Mars') — resist

2

non posse, catenam ex adamante fecit et circum
not to be able to a fetter out of steel made and around

lectum posuit, ut Martem astutia deciperet.
the bed has placed (it) that Mars with cunning he would deceive
{Mars4}

Ille cum ad constitutum venisset, concidit cum
That one when to the appointment had come has fallen together with
he fell

Venere in plagas adeo, ut se exsolvere non
Venus into the net in such a way that himself set free not

posset. Id Sol cum Vulcano nuntiasset, ille eos
he could This the Sun when to Vulcanus had reported that one them
he {is4pl}

nudos cubantes vidit. Deos omnes convocavit; qui
nude laying down has seen The gods all he has summoned who
saw

ut viderunt, riserunt. Ex eo Martem,
when they saw (it) have laughed From that (time) Mars
{Mars4}

id ne faceret, pudor terruit.
that thing that not he would do the feeling of shame has deterred
from doing that thing

3

Chapter II

THESEUS   ET   MINOS
Theseus   and   Minos

Minos	Iovis	et	Europae	filius	cum	Atheniensibus
Minos	of Iupiter	and	of Europa	son	with	the Athenians

belligeravit.	Filius	eius	Androgeus	in	pugna	est
has carried on war	Son	his	Androgeus	in	combat	is

occisus.	Qui	posteaquam	Athenienses	vicit,
killed	Which He	afterwards	the Athenians	he has defeated

vectigales	Minois	esse	coeperunt.	Instituit	autem,	ut
tributary	to Minos	to be	they have begun began	He decreed	however moreover	that

anno	unoquoque	septenos	liberos	suos	Minotauro
in year {annus5}	every single {unusquisque5}	each time seven	children	their	for the Minotaurus

ad	epulandum	mitterent.	Theseus	posteaquam	a
to	eat	they should send	Theseus	afterwards	from

Troezene	venerat	et	audiit,	quanta	calamitate	civitas
Troezen	had come came	and	has heard	by how great	a disaster	the state

afficeretur.	Inde	voluntarie	se	ad	Minotaurum
was afflicted	Thereupon	voluntarily	he himself	to	the Minotaurus

pollicitus	est	ire.	Quem	pater	cum	mitteret,	praedixit
promised	is has	to go	Whom Him	the father	when	sent	foretold told

ei,	ut,	si	victor	reverteretur,	vela	candida	in	navem
him {is3}	that	if	(as) victor	he would return	sails	white	in on	the ship

4

haberet. **Qui** **autem** **ad** **Minotaurum** **mittebantur,**
he would have — Who / They who — on the contrary — to — the Minotaurus — were sent

velis **atris** **navigabant.**
with sails — black — sailed

THESEUS APUD MINOTAURAM
Theseus — at — the Minotaurus

Theseus **posteaquam** **Cretam** **venit,** **ab** **Ariadne** **Minois**
Theseus — after — to Creta — has come / came — by — Ariadne — of Minos

filia **est** **adamatus** **adeo,** **ut** **fratrem**
the daughter — is / was — loved — so much — that — the (her) brother

proderet **et** **hospitem** **servaret.** **Ea** **enim**
delivered (to him) — and — the strange guest — saved — She — for

Theseo **monstravit** **labyrinthi** **exitum.** **Theseus** **cum**
to Theseus — has showed — of the labyrinth — the exit — Theseus — when

introisset **et** **Minotaurum** **interfecisset,** **Ariadnes**
he had gone into (it) — and — the Minotaurus — had killed — of Ariadne

monitu **licium** **revolvendo** **foras** **est** **egressus.** **Eam,**
by the counsel — a cord — by winding up — outwards — is/has — gone out — Her

quod **fidem** **ei** **dederat,** **in** **coniugio** **secum**
because — faith / solemn pledge — to her — he had given — in — marriage — with himself

habiturus, **avexit.**
(that he) would have — he took along

THESEUS ET ARIADNE
Theseus — and — Ariadne

5

Theseus in insula Dia tempestate retinebatur.
Theseus in/on the island Dia (Naxos) by a storm was retained

Cogitans, si Ariadnen in patriam portasset,
Thinking/considering if Ariadne in/to (his) home country he would have brought/bring

sibi opprobrium futurum, itaque in insula Dia
to himself disgrace (it) would be thus in/on the island Dia (Naxos)

dormientem reliquit. Eam Liber amans inde
sleeping left (her) behind Her (the god) Liber loving thereupon

sibi in coniugium abduxit. Theseus autem cum
for himself in marriage has carried away Theseus however when

navigaret, oblitus est vela atra mutare. Itaque Aegeus
he sailed forgotten is/has the sails black to change So Aegeus

pater eius, credens Theseum a Minotauro esse
father his believing Theseus by the Minotaurus to be

consumptum, in mare se praecipitavit. Ex quo
devoured into the sea himself precipitated From which

mare illud Aegeum pelagus est dictum. Ariadnes autem
sea that Aegean Sea is said/called Ariadne's however

sororem Phaedram Theseus duxit in coniugium.
sister Phaedra Theseus has led into marriage

Chapter III

OEDIPUS ET LAIUS
Oedipus and Laius

Laio Labdaci filio ab Apolline erat responsum
To Laius Labdacus' son by Apollo was answered
had been

de filii sui manu mortem ut caveret.
regarding son of his own by the hand death that he should beware of

Itaque Iocasta Menoecei filia uxor eius cum
Thus Iocasta Menoeceus' daughter wife his when

peperisset, iussit exponi. Hunc Periboea,
she had given birth he has ordered (it) to be exposed This one Periboea
Him

Polybi regis uxor, cum vestem ad mare lavaret,
Polybus of king wife when cloth at the sea she washed
{rex2} by

expositum sustulit. Polybo sciente, quod orbi
the exposed one took up Polybus knowing because bereft
With the knowledge of Polybus

erant liberis, pro suo educaverunt, eumque, quod
they were of children for their own brought (him) up and him because
{liber5pl} as

pedes transiectos haberet, Oedipum nominaverunt.
the feet perforated had Oedipus they have named
{pes1pl}

Postquam Oedipus, Laii et Iocastes filius, ad puberem
After Oedipus of Laius and of Iocaste the son at adult
to

aetatem pervenit, fortissimus praeter ceteros erat.
age has come to very strong above the others he was

Ideo / Therefore — per / through, because of — invidiam / jealousy — aequales / (his) peers — obiciebant / reproached — eum / him

subditum / a suppositious (child) — esse / to be — Polybo. / for (of) Polybus — eo / therefore — quod / that — Polybus / Polybus

tam / so — clemens / gentle — esset / was — et / and — ille / he — impudens; / insolent — quod / Which (reproach)

Oedipus / Oedipus — sensit / has felt — non / not — falso / untruly — sibi / to himself — obici. / to be thrown — Itaque / Therefor

Delphos / to (for) Delphi — est / he is has — profectus / departed — sciscitatum / for inquiring — de / about — parentibus / parents

suis. / his

Interim / In the meantime — Laio / Laius — in / in, by — prodigiis / omens — ostendebatur / was shown — mortem / death — ei / to him {is3}

adesse / to be near — de / from, by — nati / of the born one's, his son's — manu. / hand — Idem / The same He — cum / when — Delphos / to Delphi

iret, / he went — obviam / in the way to come up against, encounter — ei / to him — Oedipus / Oedipus

venit, / has come to come up against, encounter — quem / whom and him — satellites / the bodyguards — cum / when — viam / way

regi / to the king — dari / to be given — iuberent, / they ordered — neglexit. / he has ignored (it) — Rex / The king — equos / the horses

immisit / has spurred on — et / and — rota / the wheel — pedem / foot — eius / his — oppressit. / crushed — Oedipus / Oedipus

iratus inscius patrem suum de curru detraxit
angered unknowingly father his own from the chariot ~~has~~ pulled down

et occidit.
and ~~has~~ killed

OEDIPUS ET SPHINX
Oedipus and the Sphinx

Laio occiso Creon Menoecei filius regnum
Laius having been killed Creon Menouces' son the kingdom

occupavit. Interim Sphinx Typhonis in Boeotiam
took possession of In the meantime the Sphinx Typho into Boeotia

est missa, quae agros Thebanorum vexabat. Ea
is sent who the fields of the Thebans harassed She
has been laid waste

regi Creonti simultatem constituit. Si carmen, quod
to king Creon a contest ~~has~~ arranged if the song, which
riddle

posuisset, aliquis interpretatus esset, se inde
she would have posed somebody explained would be she from there
pose would have

abire; si autem datum carmen non
(would) go away if however the given riddle not

solvisset, eum se consumpturam dixit neque
he would have solved him she was to devour she ~~has~~ said and not

aliter de finibus excessuram. Rex re
otherwise from the frontiers (she) was to withdraw The king thing
territory case

audita per Graeciam edixit, qui Sphingae
having heard through Greece proclaimed (that) who the Sphinx's

9

carmen — riddle
solvisset, — would have solved / would solve
regnum — the kingdom
se — he promised
et — and
Iocasten — that

sororem — Iocaste
ei — (his) sister
in — to him
coniugium — in
daturum — marriage
promisit. — was to give

Plures — Several (men)
regni — of the kingdom
cupidine — by desire {cupido5}
venierunt — have come / came
et — and
a — by
Sphinge — the Sphinx

erant — were
consumpti. — devoured
Oedipus — Oedipus
Laii — Laius'
filius — son
venit — has come / came
et — and
carmen — the riddle

est — is / has
interpretatus. — explained
Illa — She
se — herself
praecipitavit. — precipitated
Oedipus — Oedipus

regnum — the kingdom
paternum — paternal
et — and
Iocasten — Iocaste
matrem — (his) mother
inscius — unknowingly

accepit — took
uxorem, — (as) wife
ex — from
qua — whom
procreavit — he has begotten / begot
Eteoclen — Eteocles
et — and

Polynicen, — Polynices
Antigonam — Antigone
et — and
Ismenen. — Ismene

Interim — In the meantime
Thebis — at Thebes
sterilitas — infertility
frugum — of fruits {frux2pl}
et — and
penuria — scarcity

incidit — has occurred
ob — because of
Oedipodis — Oedipus'
scelera. — misdeeds
Interrogatus — Asked

Tiresias, — Tiresias
quid — what / why
ita — so
Thebae — Thebes
vexarentur, — were (was) troubled
respondit, — he has answered
si — if

quis — somebody
ex — from
draconteo — the dragon-
genere — race
superesset — had remained
et — and
pro — for

patria — (his) home town
interiisset, — would have perished / perish
pestilentia — from the plague
liberaturum. — he was to liberate (it)

10

Tum — Then
Menoeceus, — Menoeceus
Iocastae — Iocaste's
pater, — father
se — himself
de — from
muris — the walls

praecipitavit. — precipitated
Dum — While
haec — these things
Thebis — at Thebes
geruntur, — happened
Corintho — in Corinthus

Polybus — Polybus
decedit. — passed away
Hoc — This
audito, — having heard
Oedipus — Oedipus
moleste — grievous
ferre — to carry / to be aggrieved

coepit, — began
aestimans — estimating
patrem — father
suum — his (own)
obisse. — to have died
Sed — But
eo — to him

Periboea — Periboea
de — about
eius — his
suppositione — substitution
palam — public
fecit. — has made / palam facere: disclose
Item — Likewise

Menoetes — Menoetes
senex, — an old man
qui — who
eum — him
exposuerat, — had exposed
ex — from
pedum — of the (his) feet

cicatricibus — scars
et — and
talorum — of the (his) ankles
agnovit — recognized
Lai — Laius'
filium — son

esse. — (him) to be
Oedipus — Oedipus
re — this (thing)
audita, — having heard
postquam — after
vidit — he had seen

se — he himself
tot — so great
scelera — misdeeds
nefaria — impious
fecisse, — to have done
ex — from
veste — the dress

matris — of the mother
fibulas — the pins
detraxit — has withdrawn / withdrew
et — and
se — himself
luminibus — of the light of his eyes

privavit. — -has-robbed / robbed
Regnum — The kingdom
filiis — to sons
suis — his
alternis — for alternating
annis — years

tradidit — he has surrendered
et — and
a — from
Thebis — Thebes
Antigona — with Antigone
filia — (his) daughter

duce — as a guide
profugit. — fled away

Chapter IV

HERCULIS ATHLA DUODECIM AB EURYSTHEO
Of Hercules labors (the) twelve by Eurystheus

IMPERATA
commanded

Infans cum esset, dracones duos duabus manibus
A little child when he was giant snakes two with (his) two hands

necavit. Dracones illos Iuno miserat, unde
he has killed Giant snakes those Iuno had sent Wherefor

primigenius est dictus.
"first-born" he is called

Leonem Nemaeum, quem Luna nutrierat in antro
The lion of Nemea whom the Moon had nourished in a cave

amphistomo atrotum, necavit, cuius pellem pro
with a double entrance invulnerable he has killed whose hide as

tegumento habuit.
dress he has had

Hydram Lernaeam Typhonis filiam cum capitibus
The water snake of Lerna Typho's daughter with heads

novem ad fontem Lernaeum interfecit. Haec
nine at the source of Lerna he has slayed That one
She

tantam	vim	veneni	habuit,	ut	afflatu	homines
so much	force	of venom	~~has~~ had	that	by her breath	men
such a strong venom						

necaret.	Et	si	quis	eam	dormientem	transierat,
she killed	And	if	somebody	her	while sleeping	~~had~~ passed by

vestigia	eius	afflabat	et	maiori	cruciatu
clothes	his	she breathed at	and	in greater	torment
				very great	{cruciatus5}

moriebatur.	Hanc,	Minerva	monstrante,	interfecit	et
he died	Her	Minerva	showing (how)	he ~~has~~ slayed	and
	{haec4}	{Minerva5}			

exinteravit	et	eius	felle	sagittas	suas	tinxit.
~~has~~ gutted	and	its	in vernom	arrows	his	he ~~has~~ dipped
			{fel5}			

Itaque	quicquid	postea	sagittis	fixerat,
In this way	whatever	afterwards	with the arrows	he had pierced

mortem	non	effugiebat,	unde	postea	et	ipse
death	not	escaped	whence	afterwards	and	he himself
					also	

periit	in	Phrygia.
~~has~~ perished	in	Phrygia

Aprum	Erymanthium	occidit.
The Boar	from Erymanthus	he ~~has~~ killed

Cervum	ferocem	in	Arcadia	cum	cornibus	aureis	vivum
A deer	ferocious	in	Arcadia	with	antlers	golden	alive

in	conspectu	Eurysthei	regis	adduxit.
into	the view	of Eurystheus	of the king	he ~~has~~ brought
	presence			

Aves *The birds* | **Stymphalides** *Stymphalic* | **in** *in / on* | **insula** *the island* | **Martis,** *of Mars* | **quae** *which*

emissis *pulled out* | **pennis** *with feathers* | **suis** *their own*
pulled out their feathers and used them as javelins

iaculabantur, *threw the javelins* | **sagittis** *with arrows* | **interfecit.** *he ~~has~~ slayed*
pulled out their feathers and used them as javelins

Augeae *of Augias* | **regis** *of king* | **stercus** *manure* | **bobile** *from the catttle stable* | **uno** *in one* | **die** *day* {dies5}

purgavit, *he ~~has~~ cleared away* | **maiorem** *greater* | **partem** *(for the) part* {pars4} | **Iove** *with Iupiter* | **adiutore;** *as a helper*

flumine *a river* | **ammisso** *being let in* | **totum** *all* | **stercus** *manure* | **abluit.** *it ~~has~~ washed away*

Taurum, *The bull* | **cum** *with* | **quo** *whom* | **Pasiphae** *Pasiphae* | **concubuit,** *~~has~~ slept* | **ex** *from* | **Creta** *Creta*

insula *the island* | **Mycenis** *to Mycene* | **vivum** *alive* | **adduxit.** *he ~~has~~ brought*

Diomedem *Diomedes* | **Thraciae** *of Thracia* | **regem** *the king* | **et** *and* | **equos** *horses* {equus4pl} | **quattuor** *four* | **eius,** *his*

qui *which* | **carne** *flesh* {caro5} | **humana** *human* | **vescebantur,** *fed on* | **cum** *together with* | **Abdero** *Abderus*

famulo *(his) servant* | **interfecit.** *he ~~has~~ slayed*

Hippolyten **Amazonam,** **Martis** **et** **Otrerae** **reginae**
Hippolyte / the Amazon / of Mars / and / Otrera / queen

filiam, **cui** **reginae** **Amazonis** **balteum** **detraxit;**
the daughter / to which / queen / Amazon / (her) girdle / he has taken took off

tum **Antiopam** **captivam** **Theseo** **donavit.**
then / Antiope / taken prisoner / to Theseus / ha has given gave

Geryonem **Chrysaoris** **filium** **trimembrem** **uno** **telo**
Geryon / of Chrysaor / son / with three bodies / with one / spear

interfecit.
he has killed

Draconem **immanem** **Typhonis** **filium,** **qui** **mala** **aurea**
A giant snake / enormous / of Typhon / son / who / the apples / golden

Hesperidum **servare** **solitus** **erat,** **ad** **montem** **Atlantem**
of the Hesperides / to guard / habitual habitually / was / at / Mount / Atlas

interfecit, **et** **Eurystheo** **regi** **mala** **attulit.**
he has slayed / and / to Eurystheus / king / the apples / he has brought

Canem **Cerberum** **Typhonis** **filium** **ab** **inferis**
The hound / Cerberus / of Typhon / son / from / the underworld

regi **in** **conspectum** **adduxit.**
to the king / into / the (his) view presence / he has brought

HERCULIS **PARERGA**
Of Hercules / The Additional Works

Antaeum	terrae	filium	in	Libya	occidit.	Hic	cogebat
Antaeus	of Earth	the son	in	Libya	he has killed	This one	compelled

hospites	secum	luctari	et	delassatos
(his) guests	with himself	to wrestle	and	tired / when they were tired

interficiebat;	hunc	luctando	necavit.
he killed	this one {hic4}	in wrestling	he has killed

Busiris	in	Aegypto	hospites	immolare	solitus	erat.
Busiris	in	Egypt	(his) guests	to offer in sacrifice	accustomed	was

Huius	legem	cum	audiit,	passus	est	se	cum
of this man	the law	when	he has heard	suffered	is / has	he himself	with

infula	ad	aram	adduci,	Busiris	autem	cum	vellet
a headband	to	the altar	to be led	Busiris	however	when	he wanted

deos	imprecari,	Hercules	eum	clava	ac	ministros
the gods	to invoke	Hercules	him	with a club	and	the servants

sacrorum	interfecit.
of the holy (places)	has slayed

Cygnum,	Martis	filium,	armis	superatum	occidit.
Cygnus (Swan)	Mars'	son	with weapons	overcome	he has killed

Quo	cum	Mars	venisset	et	armis
Because of what/that	when	Mars	had come / came	and	with weapons

propter	filium	contendere	vellet	cum	eo,	Iovis	inter
because of	(his) son	to contend / fight	wanted	with	him	Iupiter	between

eos	fulmen	misit.
them	(his) thunderbolt	has sent

16

Cetum, **cui** **Hesione** **fuit** **apposita,** **Troiae**
Cetus (a monster) — to whom — Hesione — has been was — put to promised — at Troy

occidit. **Laomedontem** **patrem** **Hesiones,** **quod** **eam**
he has killed — Laomedon — the father — of Hesione — because — her

non **reddebat,** **sagittis** **interfecit.**
not — he gave back — with arrows — he has slayed

Aethonem **aquilam,** **quae** **Prometheo** **cor** **exedebat,**
Aetho — the eagle — which — to Prometheus — the heart — ate out

sagittis **interfecit.**
with arrows — he has slayed

Lycum **Neptuni** **filium,** **quod** **Megaram** **Creontis** **filiam**
Lycus — Neptunus' — son — because — Megara — Creons — daughter

uxorem **eius** **et** **filios** **Therimachum** **et**
wife — his (Hercules') wife — and — (his) sons — Therimachus — and

Ophiten **occidere** **voluit,** **interfecit.**
Ophis — to kill — has wanted — he has slayed

Achelous **fluvius** **in** **omnes** **figuras** **se** **immutabat.**
Achelous — the river — into — all — shapes — himself — changed into

Hic **cum** **Hercule** **propter** **Deianirae** **coniugium** **cum**
This one — with — Hercules — because of — of Deianira's — marriage — when
He

pugnaret, **in** **taurum** **se** **convertit,** **cui** **Hercules**
fought — into — a bull — himself — has converted changed — to whom — Hercules

cornu **detraxit,** **quod** **cornu** **Hesperidibus** **sive** **Nymphis**
a horn — tore off — which — horn — to the Hesperidae — or — Nymphs

17

donavit, quod **deae** pomis **replerunt** et
he has given (and) which the goddesses with fruits filled up and
gave

cornu copiae **appellarunt.**
"horn" of plenty" called

Neleum Hippocoontis **filium** cum **decem** filiis **occidit,**
Neleus of Hippocoon son with (his) ten sons he ~~has~~ killed

quoniam is **eum** purgare **sive** lustrare
because that one him to ify or to anse by sacrifice
he

noluit tunc, **cum** Megaram, **Creontis** filiam, **uxorem**
not -has willed then when Megara Creons daughter wife

suam, et **filios** Therimachum **et** Ophiten, **interfecerat.**
his and (his) sons Therimachos and Ophis he had slayed

Eurytum, quod **Iolen** filiam **eius** in **coniugium**
Eurytus because Iole daughter his in maerriage

petiit et **ille** eum **repudiavit,** occidit.
he ~~has~~ asked and he (Eurylus) him ~~has~~ rejected he ~~has~~ killed

Centaurum Nessum, **quod** Deianiram **violare** voluit,
The Centaur Nessus because Deianira to violate he ~~has~~ wanted

occidit. Eurytionem **centaurum,** quod **Deianiram**
he ~~has~~ killed Eurytion a Centaur because Deianira

Dexameni filiam **speratam** suam **uxorem**
of Dexamenes daughter hoped for his wife

petiit, occidit.
~~has~~ requested (in marriage) he ~~has~~ killed

18

HERCULES ET NESSUS
Hercules and Nessus

Nessus, Ixionis et Nubis filius, centaurus, rogatus
Nessus of Ixion and Nubis the son a Centaur (was) requested

ab Deianira, ut se flumen Euhenum transferret.
by Deianira that her the river Eufrates he would bear across

Quam, sublatam in flumine ipso, violare voluit.
Whom when brought down in the river itself to violate ~~has~~ wanted

Hoc Hercules cum intervenisset et Deianira cum
Therefore Hercules when he had come by and Deianira when
came by

fidem eius implorasset, Nessum sagittis confixit.
faith/help his ~~had~~ begged for Nessus with arrows ~~has~~ transfixed

Ille moriens, cum sciret sagittas hydrae Lernaeae
He dying when he knew the arrows of the water snake of Lernae

felle tinctas quantam vim haberent veneni,
with the venom sprinkled how much force had of venom
how venomous were

sanguinem suum exceptum Deianirae dedit et id
blood his own taken out to Deianira has given and it
collected gave

philtrum esse dixit; si vellet, ne se
a love-potion to be ~~has~~ said If she should wish that not her

coniunx sperneret, eo iuberet vestem eius
(her) husband spurned with it he commanded clothes his

perungi. Id Deianira credens conditum diligenter
to be anointed This Deianira believing hidden diligently

servavit.
conserved

19

MEGARA
Megara

Hercules ad canem tricipitem erat missus ab
Hercules — to — the dog — with three heads — was — sent — by

Eurystheo rege. Lycus, Neptuni filius, putabat eum
Eurystheus — the king — Lycus — of Neptunus — son — thought — him

periisse, deinde Megaram, Creontis filiam, uxorem
to have perished — then — Megara — of Creon — daughter — wife

eius, et filios Therimachum et Ophiten interficere
his — and — (his) sons — Therimachus — and — Ophis — to slay

voluit et regnum occupare. Hercules eo intervenit
has wanted — and — the kingdom — to occupy — Hercules — him — came upon

et Lycum interfecit; postea ab Iunone insania
and — Lycus — he has slayed — thereafter — by — Iuno — with insanity

obiecta Megaram et filios Therimachum et
having been afflicted — Megara — and — (his) sons — Therimachus — and

Ophiten interfecit. Postquam suae mentis compos est
Ophis — he has slayed — After — of his — mind {mens2} — in control of — he is / has

factus, ab Apolline petiit dari sibi
made / become — from — Apollo — he has asked — to be given — to himself {se3}

responsum, quomodo scelus purgaret. Apollo sortem
an answer / oracle — in which way — the crime — he would purge — Apollo — an oracle

reddere noluit, itaque Hercules iratus de fano
to give — not has willed — and therefore — Hercules — angry — from — temple

eius tripodem sustulit. Quem postea Iovis iussu
his — the tripod — has carried away — Which — afterwards — of Iupiter — by order

reddidit	et	nolentem	sortem	dare
he has given gave back	and	the not willing (Apollo)	an oracle	to give

iussit.	Hercules	ob	id	a	Mercurio
he (Iupiter) ordered	Hercules	because of	this	by	Mercurius

Omphalae	reginae	in	servitutem	datus	est.
to Omphala	queen	into	slavery	given	is has been

Chapter V

ALEXANDER PARIS
Alexander   Paris

Priamus,	Laomedontis	filius,	cum	complures	liberos
Priamus	of Laomedon	son	when	several	children (sons)

haberet	ex	concubitu	Hecubae.	Uxor	eius
he had	from	sexual relationship	with Hecuba.	(his) wife	his

praegnans	in	quiete	vidit	se	facem	ardentem
being pregnant	in	rest/sleep	has seen / saw	herself	torch	a burning

parere,	ex	qua	serpentes	plurimos	exisse.	Id
give birth to	out of	which	snakes	very many	to go out from / went out	This

visum	omnibus	coniectoribus	cum	narratum	esset,
vision	to all	diviners	when	told	it was

imperant,	quicquid	pareret,	necaret,
they order (that)	whatever	she would give birth to	should she kill

ne	id	patriae	exitio	foret.
in order that not	it	of his home town	to the destruction	would be

Postquam	Hecuba	peperit	Alexandrum,	datur
After	Hecuba	has given birth to	Alexander	he was given

interficiendus,	quem	satellites	misericordia	exposuerunt.
to be killed	which but him	the attendants	out of compassion	have exposed

Eum	pastores	pro	suo	filio	repertum	expositum
Him	herdsmen	instead of as	their own	son	having found	the exposed one

educarunt	eumque	Parim	nominaverunt.
have brought up	and him	Paris	have named

22

Is / This one/He   **cum** / when   **ad** / to   **puberem** / adult   **aetatem** / age   **pervenisset,** / he had come   **habuit** / has had / was fond of

taurum / a bull   **in** / among   **deliciis.** / those he was fond of / was fond of   **Cum** / When   **venissent** / had come / came   **satellites** / attendants

missi / sent   **a** / by   **Priamo,** / Priamus   **ut** / in order that   **taurum** / a bull   **aliquis** / somebody   **adduceret,** / would bring along

qui / that it   **in** / in   **athlo** / the athletic contest   **funebri,** / at the funeral   **quod** / which   **ei** / for him (Paris)

fiebat, / was made / held   **poneretur,** / would be placed / offered   **coeperunt** / they have begun / began   **Paridis** / of Paris   **taurum** / the bull

abducere. / to carry off.   **Qui** / Who / But he   **persecutus** / pursued   **est** / is / has   **eos** / them   **et** / and   **inquisivit,** / has inquiredd   **quo** / why

eum / it   **ducerent;** / they lead away   **illi** / they   **indicant** / indicate   **se** / that they   **eum** / it   **ad** / to   **Priamum** / Priamus

adducere / bring   **ei,** / for him   **qui** / who   **vicisset** / would have won   **ludis** / the games   **funebribus** / funeral

Alexandri. / of Alexander   **Ille** / That one / He   **amore** / by love   **incensus** / incited   **tauri** / of the bull   **sui** / his own

descendit / has descended   **in** / into   **certamen** / the contest   **et** / and   **omnia** / all (contests)   **vicit,** / he has won   **fratres** / brothers

quoque / too   **suos** / his own   **superavit.** / he has surpassed / surpassed   **Indignans** / Indignant   **Deiphobus** / Deiphobus   **gladium** / a sword

ad / to   **eum** / him   **strinxit;** / has drawn / drew   **at** / but   **ille** / he   **in** / to   **aram** / the altar   **Iovis** / of Iupiter   **Hercei** / Herceus

insiluit. / has leapt   **Cum** / When   **Cassandra** / Cassandra   **vaticinaretur** / prophesied   **eum** / him / that he was   **fratrem** / (her) brother

esse, / to be / that he was   **Priamus** / Priamus   **eum** / him   **agnovit** / has recognized   **regiaque** / and in the palace   **recepit.** / has received

TROIA - EQUUS TROIANUS
Troy   The Horse   Trojan

Achivi   cum   per   decem   annos   Troiam   capere   non
The Greeks   when   during   ten   years   Troy   capture   not

possent,   Epeus   monitu   Minervae   equum   mirae
could   Epeus   by the counsel   of Minerva   a horse   of marvelous

magnitudinis   ligneum   fecit   eoque   sunt   collecti
size   wooden   has made   and in it   are have   gathered

Menelaus   Ulixes   et   heroes   septem   alii.   Et   in   equo
Menelaus   Odysseus   and   heroes   seven   other   And   in on   the horse

scripserunt   DANAI   MINERVAE   DONO   DANT,
they have written wrote   The Danaeans (Greeks)   To Minerva   as a gift   give

castraque   transtulerunt   Tenedo.   Id   Troiani   cum
and (their) camp   they have moved   to Tenedos   This   the Trojans   when

viderunt   arbitrati   sunt   hostes   abisse;   Priamus
have seen saw   supposed   they are have   the enemy   to have gone away   Priamus

equum   in   arcem   Minervae   duci   imperavit,
the horse   into   the citadel   of (built by) Minerva   to be dragged   has ordered

feriatique   magno   opere   ut   essent,   edixit;   id
and celebrations   with great   labor outlay   that   there would be   has ordained   This

vates   Cassandra   cum   vociferaretur   inesse   hostes,
the prophetess   Cassandra   when   she cried out   to be therein   enemies

fides   ei   habita   non   est.
faith   to her   had/given   not   is

Quem in arcem cum statuissent et ipsi noctu
Which into the citadel when they had placed and in the same night
And it

lusu atque vino lassi obdormissent, Achivi ex
by play and by wine weary they had fallen asleep the Greeks out of

equo aperto a Sinone exierunt et portarum
the horse opened by Sinon have gone out and of the gates
went out

custodes occiderunt sociosque signo dato
the guards ~~have~~ killed and (their) comrades the sign having been given

receperunt et Troia sunt potiti.
they ~~have~~ received and Troy are seized
let in have

ACHILLES
Achilles

Thetis Nereis rescivit Achillem filium suum, quem
Thetis the Nereid has come (that) Achilles son her whom
came to know

ex Peleo habebat, si ad Troiam expugnandam
from Peleus she had if to Troy to conquer

isset, periturum. Ideo commendavit eum in
he would have gone was to perish Therefore she committed him to
went

insulam Scyron ad Lycomedem regem, quem ille inter
the island Skyros to Lycomedes king whom he among
and him

virgines filias habitu femineo servabat nomine
the maidens daughters in dress woman's kept with a name

mutato. Nam virgines Pyrrham nominarunt, quoniam
changed For the maidens Pyrrha ~~have~~ named (him) because

capillis flavis fuit et Graece rufum "pyrrhon"
with hairs / blond / he has been / and / in Greek / red-haired / "pyrrhon"
was -haired / / was -haired

dicitur.
is said / called

Achivi autem cum rescissent ibi eum
The Greeks / however / when / they had come to know / there / him

occultari, ad regem Lycomeden oratores miserunt, qui
to be hidden / to / king / Lycomedon / speakers, envoys / have sent / who

rogarent, ut eum adiutorium Danais mitteret.
should ask / that / him / (as) support / for the Greeks / he would send

Rex cum negaret apud se esse, potestatem
The king / when / denied / at, in his house / him(self) / (him) to be / authority

eis fecit, ut in regia quaererent. Sed
to them / has made, gave / that, to search / in / the palace / thay would search, to search / But

intellegere non poterant, quis esset eorum.
find out / not / they could / who / he would be/was / of them

Ulixes in regio vestibulo munera feminea posuit,
Odysseus / in / the royal / entrance-court / accessories / feminine / placed

in quibus clipeum et hastam, et subito tubicinem
among / which / a shield / and / a spear / and / suddenly / the tuba

iussit canere armorumque crepitum et clamorem
he has ordered / to play / and of weapons / the clattering / and / the rumour

fieri iussit. Achilles hostem arbitrans adesse
to be made / he has ordered / Achilles / an enemy / believing / to be there

vestem muliebrem dilaniavit atque clipeum et hastam
(his) dress / feminine / has torn, tore up / and / the shield / and / the spear

26

arripuit. Ex hoc est cognitus, suasque operas
~~has~~ grabbed From this he is been known and his efforts
has

Argivis promisit et milites Myrmidones.
to the Greeks ~~has~~ promised and the soldiers Myrmidonian

PARIDIS IUDICIUM
Of Paris the Judgment

Iovis cum Thetis Peleo nuberet, ad epulum dicitur
Iupiter when Thetis with Peleus married at the banquet it is said

omnis deos convocasse excepta Eride, id
all the gods to have assembled with the exception of Eris that

est Discordia. Quae cum postea supervenisset nec
is Discord Who when afterwards she had come up and not

admitteretur ad epulum, ab ianua misit in medium
was admittted to the banquet through the door sent in the middle
threw

malum. Dicit, quae esset formosissima, attolleret.
an apple She says who would be the most beautiful would take it
was

Iuno, Venus, Minerva formam sibi vindicare
Iuno Venus Minerva beauty for herself to vindicate

coeperunt, inter quas magna discordia orta. Iovis
have begun among whom great discord has sprung up Iupiter
began)

imperat Mercurio, ut deducat eas in Ida monte ad
commands to Mercurius that he leads away them on Ida Mount to

Alexandrum Paridem eumque iubeat iudicare.
Alexander Paris and him he orders to give judgment

Cui	Iuno,	si	secundum	se	iudicasset,
To this one him	Iuno	if	in favour of	herself	he would have judged

pollicita	est	in	omnibus	terris	eum	regnaturum,	divitem
promised	is has	in	all	lands	he	was to reign	rich

praeter	ceteros	praestaturum.	Minerva,	si	inde
beyond	the others	was to stand out	Minerva	if	from there

victrix	discederet,	fortissimum	inter	mortales	futurum
as victrix	she would depart	the strongest	among	the mortals	he was to be

spopondit,	et	omni	artificio	scium.	Venus	autem
has given gave pledge	and	in every	craft	skilled	Venus	however

Helenam	Tyndarei	filiam	formosissimam	omnium
Helena	of Tyndareus	the daughter	the most beautiful	of all

mulierum	se	in	coniugium	dare	promisit.	Paris	donum
women {mulier2pl}	him	in	marriage	to give	has promised	Paris	gift

posterius	prioribus	anteposuit,	Veneremque
the last	to the former	has placed before valued above	and Venus

pulcherrimam	esse	iudicavit.	Ob	id	Iuno	et
the most fair	to be	he has judged	Because of	that	Iuno	and

Minerva	Troianis	fuerunt	infestae.	Alexander	Veneris
Minerva	to the Trojans	have been were	inimical	Alexander	of Venus

impulsu	Helenam	a	Lacedaemone	ab	hospite
on the instigation	Helena	from	Lacedaemon (Sparta)	from	his host

Menelao	Troiam	abduxit	eamque	in	coniugio	habuit
Menelaos	to Troy	has carried away	and her	in	marriage	has had

cum	ancillis	duabus	Aethra	et	Thisadie,	quas	Castor
with	servants	two	Aethra	and	Thisadie	whom	Castor

et	Pollux	captivas	ei	assignarant,	aliquando	reginas.
and	Pollux	as prisoners	to him	had assigned	once	queens

Chapter VI

ODYSSEUS
Odysseus

Agamemnon	et	Menelaus	Atrei	filii	cum	ad	Troiam
Agamemnon	and	Menelaus	of Atreus	the sons	when	to	Troy

oppugnandam	coniuratos	duces	ducerent,	in	insulam
to conquer (it)	sworn together	the leaders	led	to	the island

Ithacam	ad	Ulixem	Laertis	filium	venerunt.	Illo
ithaca	at	Odysseus	of Laertes	the son	have come / came	To him

fuit	responsum,	si	ad	Troiam	isset,	post
has been / was	responded (by an oracle)	if	to	Troy	he would go	after

vicesimum	annum	solum	sociis	perditis	egentem
the twentieth	year	alone	his comrades	having lost	destitute

domum	rediturum.	Itaque	cum	sciret	ad	se
to house/home	he was to return	Therefore	when	he knew	to	him

oratores	venturos,	insaniam	simulans	pileum	sumpsit
messengers	were to come	insanity	pretending	a fool's cap	has taken / took

et	equum	cum	bove	iunxit	ad	aratrum.	Quem
and	a horse	with	an oxen	has attached	to	the plough	Whom / But him

Palamedes	ut	vidit,	sensit	simulare.	Telemachum,
Palamedes	when	he has seen / saw	has felt	to pretend	Telemachus

filium	eius,	cunis	subtulit,	inde	aratro
son	his	from the cradle	he has taken / took away	thereupon	(before) the plough

ei	subiecit	et	ait	"Simulatione
to him (Odysseus)	laid down	and	said	Feigning

deposita (having been put away) inter (among) coniuratos (the sworn together) veni." (come) Tunc (Then) Ulixes (Odysseus) fidem (faith/oath) dedit (has given / gave) se (that he) venturum; (was to come) ex (From) eo (that) Palamedi (to Palamedes) infestus (inimical) fuit. (he has been / was)

ODYSSEA
The Odyssee

Ulixes (Odysseus) cum (when) ab (from) Ilio (Ilium (Troy)) in (to) patriam ((his) native country) Ithacam (Ithaca) rediret, (went back) tempestate (by a storm) ad (to) Ciconas (the Cicones) est (is) delatus. (carried away) Eorum (Their {is2pl}) oppidum (town) Ismarum (Ismarus) expugnavit (he ~~has~~ conquered) praedamque (and the booty) sociis (to his companions) distribuit. (he ~~has~~ distributed)

Inde (From there) ad (to) Lotophagos, (the Lotuseaters) homines (people) minime (not in the least) malos, (bad) qui (who) loton (the lotus) ex (from) foliis (the leaves / petals) florem (of the flower) procreatum (produced) edebant. (ate) Id (That) cibi (of food) genus (kind) tantam (so great a) suavitatem (sweetness) praestabat, (supplied) ut, (that) qui (those who) gustabant, (tasted (it)) oblivionem (forgetfulness / to become forgetful of) caperent (took) domum (to the house / home) reditionis. (of going back) Ad (To)

30

eos — them
socii — companions
duo — two
missi — sent
ab — by
Ulixe — Odysseus
cum — when
gustarent — they tasted

herbas — the weeds
ab — by
eis — them
datas, — given
ad — to
naves — the ships
obliti — forgotten
sunt — are / have
reverti, — to go back

quos — whom / and them
vinctos — bound
ipse — he
reduxit. — has led back

Inde — From there
ad — (he came) to
Cyclopem — the Cyclops
Polyphemum — Polyphemus
Neptuni — of Neptunus
filium. — son

Huic — To him
responsum — answered
erat — was / had been
ab — by
augure — the diviner
Telemo — Telemus
Eurymi — of Eurymus

filio, {filius5} — the son
ut — that
caveret, — he should take care
ne — that not
ab — by
Ulixe — Odysseus

excaecaretur. — he would be blinded
Hic — This one
media fronte — middle forehead / in the centre of his forehead
unum — one
oculum — eye

habebat — had
et — and
carnem — flesh
humanam — human
epulabatur. — fed imself on
Postquam — After

pecus — the flock
in — into
speluncam — the cave
redegerat, — he had driven back
molem — boulder
saxeam — rocky

ingentem — an enormous
ad — at
ianuam — the entrance
opponebat. — placed in the way
Qui — Who / And he
Ulixem — Odysseus

cum — together with
sociis — (his) companions
inclusit — has enclosed
sociosque — and companions
eius — his

consumere — consume
coepit. — began / has begun
Ulixes — Odysseus
videbat — saw
eius — his
immanitati {immanitas3} — to the enormous size

atque — and
feritati — savageness
resistere — resist
se — he himself
non — not
posse. — to be able / could
Ideo — Therefore

31

vino | quod | a | Marone | acceperat | eum | inebriavit,
with wine | which | from | Maron | he had received | him | ~~has~~ made drunk

seque | "Utin" | vocari | dixit. | Deinde | oculum | eius
and himself | "Utis" | to be called | ~~has~~ said | Thereupon | eye | his

trunco | ardenti | exureret. | Ille | clamore | suo
with a tree trunk | glowing | he burnt out | That one / He | by outcry | his

ceteros | Cyclopas | convocavit | eisque
the other | Cyclops | ~~has~~ called together | and to them

spelunca | praeclusa | dixit: | "Utis | me | excaecat." | Illi,
the cave / while the cave was blocked | having been blocked | ~~has~~ said | "Utis" | me | blinds | They

credentes | eum | deridendi | gratia | dicere, | neglexerunt.
believing | (that) he | to make fun / with the purpose of... | grace | to say | did nothing about (it)

At | Ulixes | socios | suos | ad | pecora | alligavit | et | ipse
But | Odysseus | companions | his | to | the sheep | bound | and | he

se | ad | arietem | et | ita | exierunt.
himself | to | the ram | and | in that way | they have gone out

Ulixes | ad | Aeolum, | Hellenis | filium, | navigabat. | Illo | ab
Odysseus | to | Aeolus | of Helle | the son | sailed | To him | by

Iove | ventorum | potestas | fuit | tradita. | Is
Iupiter | of the winds | the power (over) | had been | handed over | This one / He

Ulixem | hospitio | libere | accepit | follesque | ventorum
Odysseus | with hospitality | liberally | ~~has~~ received | and bags | of the winds

ei | plenos | muneri | dedit. | Socii | vero | aurum
full/filled | to him | present / gave as a present | has given | The companions | however | gold

argentumque | esse | crederunt, | et | secum
and silver | (it) to be | believed | and | with themselves

partiri voluerunt. Folles clam solverunt
(it) to be shared have wanted The bags in secret they have opened

ventique evolaverunt. Rursum ad Aeolum est delatus,
and the winds have flown Back to Aeolus he is carried
flew away

a quo eiectus est, quod videbatur Ulixes
by whom thrown out he is because was seen/seemed Odysseus

numen deorum infestum habere.
divine (will) of the gods hostile to have

Inde venit ad Laestrygonas, quorum rex fuit
From there he has come to the Laestrygones whose king has been
came was

Antiphates, qui capto homine a Ulixe praetermisso
Antiphates who being seized the man by Odysseus sent ahead

eum devoravit. Laestrygonae naves undecim confregerunt
him devoured The Laestrygones ships eleven have smashed

et omnes qui in eis erant devorabant, una excepta
and all who in them were devoured one excepted

nave qua, sociis eius consumptis, evasit in
ship with which companions his having been eaten he has escaped to

insulam Aenariam.
the island Aenaria

Hinc habitabat Circe, Solis filiam, quae
Here dwelled Circe of the Sun daughter who

potione data homines in feras bestias
a potion having been given men into wild beasts
after giving (them) a potion

33

commutabat. **Ad** **quam** **Eurylochum** **cum** **viginti** **duobus**
changed — To — whom — Eurylochus — with — twenty — two

sociis **misit,** **quos** **illa** **ab** **humana** **specie**
companions — he ~~has~~ sent — whom — she — from — a human — appearance

immutavit. **Eurylochus** **timens,** **qui** **non** **intraverat,**
~~has~~ transformed — Eurylochus — fearing — who — not — had come in

inde **fugit** **et** **Ulixi** **nuntiavit.** **Ille** **solus**
from there — - has- fled — and — to Odysseus — reported — This one/He — alone

ad **eam** **se** **contulit.** **Sed** **in** **itinere** **Mercurius** **ei**
to — her — ~~himself~~ — brought / went — But — in / on — the road — Mercurius — to him

remedium **dedit** **monstravitque,** **quomodo** **Circen**
an antidote — has given / gave — and ~~has~~ showed — in which way — Circe

deciperet. **Postea** **ad** **Circen** **venit** **et** **poculum**
he would deceive — After that — to — Circe — he has come / came — and — a bowl

ab **ea** **accepit,** **remedium** **Mercurii** **monitu**
from — her — ~~has~~ received — the antidote — of Mercurius — on the advice

coniecit. **Deinde** **ensem** **strinxit,** **minatus,** **nisi**
put into (it) — Thereupon — (his) sword — he ~~has~~ unsheated — threatening — if not

socios **sibi** **restitueret,** **se** **eam** **interfecturum.**
the companions — to him — she would give back — he — her — was to kill

Tunc **Circe** **intellexit** **non** **sine** **voluntate** **deorum** **id**
Then — Circe — ~~has~~ understood — not — without — the will — of the gods — this

esse **factum;** **itaque** **fide** **data** **se** **nihil**
to be have — happened — therefore — faith/an oath — having been given — she — nothing

tale **commissuram** **socios** **eius** **ad** **pristinam** **formam**
such — was to commit — companions — his — to — (their) former — shape

34

restituit. (has restored) **Et** (And) **ipsa** (she herself) **cum** (with) **eodem** (the same him) **concubuit,** (slept together) **ex** (out of) **quo** (which)

filios (sons) **duos** (two) **procreavit,** (she has produced) **Nausithoum** (Nausithous) **et** (and) **Telegonum.** (Telegonus)

Inde (From there) **proficiscitur** (he departs) **ad** (to) **lacum** (Lake) **Avernum,** (Avernus) **ad** (to) **inferos** (the underworld)

descendit, (he has descended) **ibique** (and there) **invenit** (has found) **Elpenorem,** (Elpenor) **socium** (companion) **suum,** (his)

quem (whom) **ad** (at) **Circen** (Circe) **reliquerat.** (he had left behind) **Interrogavit** (He has interrogated) **eum,** (him)

quomodo (in which way) **eo** (there) **pervenisset.** (he had arrived) **Elpenor** (Elpenor) **respondit** (has answered) **se** (he)

ebrium (being drunk) **per** (by/from) **scalam** (the stairs) **cecidisse** (to have fallen) **et** (and) **cervices** ((his) neck)

fregisse. (to have broken) **Et** (And) **deprecatus** (entreated) **est** (he is/has) **eum,** (him) **cum** (when) **ad** (to)

superos (the upper world) **rediret,** (he would return) **se** (him) **sepulturae** (to a grave) **traderet** (would bequeath) **et** (and)

sibi (for him) **in** (upon) **tumulo** ((his) mound) **gubernaculum** (a rudder) **poneret.** (would place) **Ibi** (There) **et** (also)

cum (with) **matre** ((his) mother) **Anticlia** (Anticlia) **est** (he is/has) **locutus** (spoken) **de** (about) **fine** (the end)

errationis (of wandering) **suae.** (his) **Deinde** (Thereupon) **ad** (to) **superos** (the upper world) **reversus** (returned)

35

Elpenorem (Elpenor) **sepelivit** (he has buried) **et** (and) **gubernaculum** (a rudder) **ita,** (such) **ut** (as) **rogaverat,** (he had asked)

in (upon) **tumulo** (the mound) **ei** (for him) **fixit.** (he has attached)

Tum (The) **ad** (to) **Sirenas** (the Sirens) **venit,** (he has come / came) **quae** (who) **partem** (part) **superiorem** (the upper)

muliebrem (of a woman) **habebant,** (had) **inferiorem** (the lower (part)) **autem** (however) **gallinaceam.** (of a chicken)

Harum (Whose) **fatum** (fate) **fuit** (it has been / was) **tam** (so) **diu** (long (a time)) **vivere,** (to live) **quam** (as)

diu (-long (time) as-) **earum** (their) **cantum** (song) **mortalis** (mortal (man)) **audiens** (hearing) **nemo** (nobody / no)

praetervectus (sailed by) **esset.** (would be have) **Ulixes** (Odysseus) **monitus** (warned) **a** (by) **Circe** (Circe) **Solis** (of the Sun)

filia (daughter) **sociis** (at his companions) **cera** (with wax) **aures** (the ears) **obturavit** (has plugged) **seque** (and himself) **ad** (to)

arborem (the tree / mast) **malum** (mast) **constringi** (to be bound) **iussit** (has ordered) **et** (and) **sic** (so) **praetervectus** (sailed by)

est. (is / has)

Inde (From there) **ad** (to) **Scyllam,** (Scylla) **Typhonis** (Typho's) **filiam,** (daughter) **venit,** (he has come / came) **quae** (who)

superiorem (the upper) **corporis** (of the body) **partem** (part) **muliebrem,** (as a woman) **inferiorem** (the lower) ab (downwards) from — inguine the groin {inguen5} — piscis, of a fish — et and — sex six — canes dogs seals — ex out of — se herself

natos born — habebat. had — Ea She — sex six — socios companions — Ulixis of Odysseus — nave from the ship

abreptos having been snatched away — consumpsit. ~~has~~ consumed

In To — insulam the island — Siciliam (of) Sicily — ad to — Solis of the Sun — pecus flock — sacrum sacred — venerat, he has come came

quod that — Tiresias Tiresias — vetuerit had forbidden — violari. to be violated — Sed But — cum when — Ulixes Odysseus

condormiret fell asleep — socii the companions — involarunt rushed upon — pecus, the flock — quod which — socii companions

eius, his — fame by hunger — pressi, pressed — cum when — coquerent, they cooked (it) — carnes the meats — ex out of

aeneo the copper kettle — dabant gave — balatus. bleating

Ad To — Charybdin Charybdis — perlatus, (he is) carried — quae who — ter three times — die on a day

obsorbebat swallowed (water) — terque and three times — eructabat. threw (it) up — Eam Her — monitu by the warning

Tiresiae of Tiresias — praetervectus he sailed by — est. is has — Sed But — Sol the Sun — iratus, (was) angered — quod because

37

pecus	eius	erat	violatum.	Ob	id	Iovis	navem	eius
flock	his	was	violated	Because of	this	Iupiter	ship	his

fulmine	incendit.
with lightning	has put on fire

Ex	his	locis	errans	naufragio	facto	sociis
From	these	places	wandering	shipwreck	having made	(his) companions

amissis	enatavit	in	insulam	Ogygiam,	ubi
having lost	he escaped by swimming	to	the island	Ogygia	where

habitabat	Calypso	Atlantis	filia,	nympha.	Ea	specie
dwelled	Calypso	Atlas'	daughter	a nymph	She	by the looks

Ulixis	capta,	anno	toto	eum	retinuit	neque
of Odysseus	captivated	during a year	whole	him	has retained	and not

a	se	dimittere	voluit,	donec	Mercurius	Iovis
from	herself	let go	has willed	until	Mercurius	of Iupiter

iussu	denuntiavit	nymphae,	ut	eum	dimitteret.
on the command	has given gave notice	to the nymph	that	him	she should let go

Et	ibi	facta	rate	Calypso	omnibus	rebus
And	there	having been made	a raft	Calypso	with all	things

ornatum	eum	dimisit.
provided	him	has let go

Eam	ratim	Neptunus	fluctibus	disiecit,	quod
That	raft	Neptunus	by the waves	dashed to pieces	because

Cyclopem	filium	eius	lumine	privaverat.	Ibi	cum
the Cyclops	son	his	of the light	he had robbed	There	when

fluctibus iactaretur, Leucothoe, quam nos
by the waves he was driven hither and thither Leucothoe whom we

Matrem Matutam dicimus, quae in mari exigit
the Mother Great say/call who in the sea spends

aevum, balteum ei dedit, quo sibi
time everlasting a girdle to him has given that with that to himself
gave {= ut eo}

pectus suum vinciret, ne pessum abiret.
breast his he would gird that not downwards he would go away

Quod cum fecisset, enatavit.
That when he had done he has escaped by swimming

Inde in insulam Phaeacum venit nudusque ex
Thereupon to the island of the Phaeaces he has come and nude from
came

arborum foliis se obruit, qua Nausicaa
of trees the leaves himself covered there where Nausicaa

Alcinoi regis filia vestem ad flumen lavandam
of Alcinous the king daughter cloth to the river to be washed
{rex2} clothes

tulit. Ille erepsit e foliis et ab ea petit,
brought He has crawled out of the leaves and from her he has asked

ut sibi opem ferret. Illa misericordia mota
that him help she would bring That one/She by pity moved
would give help

pallio eum operuit et ad patrem suum eum
with a cloak him covered and to father her him

adduxit. Alcinous hospitio liberaliter acceptum
led Alcinous with hospitality liberally (him) having received

donisque — and with gifts
decoratum — honoured
in — to
patriam — (his) home country
Ithacam — Ithaca
dimisit. — sent away

Ira — By the wrath
Mercurii — of Mercurius
iterum — again
naufragium — shipwreck
fecit — he has made suffered

Post — After
vicesimum — the twentieth
annum — year
sociis — (his) companions
amissis — having lost
solus — alone
in — to

patriam — (his) home country
redit, — he has come came back
et — and
cum — when
ab — by
hominibus — the men people

ignoraretur — not recognized
domumque — and house
suam — his own
attigisset, — had reached
procos, — the suitors
qui — who

Penelopen — Penelope
in — in
coniugium — marriage
petebant, — sought (to obtain)
obsidentes — besetting
vidit — he has seen saw

regiam — the palace
seque — and himself
hospitem — a guest
simulavit. — has feigned (to be)
Et — And
Euryclia — Euryclia

nutrix — wet nurse
ipsius, — his
dum — while
pedes — the feet
ei — him
lavat, — washed
ex — from
cicatrice — a scar

Ulixem — Odysseus
esse — (him) to be
cognovit. — has known knew
Postea — After that
procos — the suitors
Minerva — Minerva

adiutrice — being (his) helper
cum — together with
Telemacho — Telemachus
filio — (his) son
et — and
duobus — two

servis — servants
interfecit — he has killed
sagittis. — with arrows

Chapter VII

CURA, AUT UNDE ORTA VOX "HOMO"
Cura — or — from where — came up — the word — "homo"

Cura cum quendam fluvium transiret, vidit
Cura (goddess of "concern") — when — some — river — she crossed — she has seen / saw

cretosum lutum, sustulit cogitabunda et coepit fingere
chalky — clay — took (it) up — thoughtfully — and — has begun / began — to knead

hominem. Dum deliberat secum quidnam fecisset,
(a) man — While — she pondered — by herself — wat then — she had made

intervenit Iovis. Rogat eum Cura, ut ei daret
has intervened — Iupiter — Asks — to him — Cura, — that — to it — he may give

spiritum, quod facile ab Iove impetravit. Cui cum
spirit — which — easily — from — Iupiter — she has obtained — To whom — when

vellet Cura nomen suum imponere, Iovis prohibuit
wanted — Cura — name — her own — to impose / assign — Iupiter — has forbidden / forbade (it)

suumque nomen ei dandum esse dixit. Dum de
and his own — name — to it — to be given — to be / was — has said — While — about

nomine Cura et Iovis disceptarent, surrexit et Tellus
the name — Cura — and — Iupiter — debated — has come / came up — also — Tellus / Earth

suumque nomen ei imponi debere dicebat,
and his own — name — to it — be assigned — must — said

quandoquidem corpus suum praebuisset. Sumpserunt
since — body — his own — he had provided — They have taken / took

Saturnum iudicem; quibus Saturnus aequus videtur
Saturnus — as a judge — To whom / To them — Saturnus — just — was seen / seemed

41

iudicasse: "Tu, Iovis, quoniam spiritum dedisti,
to have judged You Iupiter because the spirit you have given

animam post mortem accipe. Tellus, quoniam corpus
the soul after death receive Tellus because the body

praebuit, corpus recipito. Cura quoniam prima eum
he has provided the body receive Cura because first him
get

finxit, quamdiu vixerit, Cura eum possideat. Sed
kneaded as long as has lived Cura him let possess But

quoniam de nomine eius controversia est, homo
because about name his a quarrel is "homo"
exists

vocetur, quoniam ex humo videtur esse factus."
let him be called because out of humus he is seen to be made
earth

DEUCALION ET PYRRHA
Deucalion and Pyrrha

Cataclysmus, quod nos diluvium vel irrigationem dicimus,
The great flood which we "diluvium" or "irrigation" say
call

cum factum est, omne genus humanum interiit
when happened is all kind human has perished
has mankind

praeter Deucalionem et Pyrrham, qui in montem
except Deucalion and Pyrrha who upon Mount

Aetnam, qui altissimus in Sicilia esse dicitur, fugerunt.
Etna which the highest in Sicily to be is said have fled

Hi propter solitudinem cum vivere non possent,
These because of the solitude when live not they could
They

42

petierunt ab Iove, ut aut homines daret aut
have requested from Iupiter that either men he would give or

eos pari calamitate afficeret. Tum Iovis iussit
them with an equal disaster would afflict Then Iupiter has ordered

eos lapides post se iactare; quos Deucalion
them stones behind themselves to throw Those which Deucalion

iactavit, viros esse iussit, quos Pyrrha,
has thrown men to be he has ordered those which Pyrrha
threw

mulieres. Ob eam rem "laos" dictus, "laas"
women Because of that thing "laos" is said "laas"
cause Greek for "people" people say

enim Graece lapis dicitur.
for in Greek "stone" is called

EUROPA
Europa

Europa Argiopes et Agenoris filia. Hanc
Europa of Argiope and of Agenor (was the) daughter Her

Iuppiter in taurum conversus a Sidone Cretam
Iupiter into a bull being transformed from Sidon to Creta

transportavit et ex ea procreavit Minoem,
has carried across and from her he has begotten Minos

Sarpedonem, Rhadamanthum. Huius pater Agenor
Sarpedon Rhadamanthus Of this one father Agenor
Her

suos filios misit, ut sororem reducerent aut
his sons sent that (their) sister they would bring back or
{suus4pl}

43

ipsi — in — suum — conspectum — non — redirent.
themselves — to — his — sight — not — they would come back

Phoenix — in — Africam — est — profectus, — ibique — remansit;
Phoenix — to — Africa — is / has — departed — and there — has remained

inde — Afri — Poeni — sunt — appellati. — Cilix — suo
thence / that's why — the Africans — "Phoenicians" — are — called — Cilix — with his

nomine — Ciliciae — nomen — indidit. — Cadmus — cum — erraret,
name {nomen5} — to Cilicia — a name — conferred — Cadmus — when — he wandered

Delphos — devenit. — Ibi — responsum — accepit, — ut — a
at Delphi — has arrived — There — an answer / oracle — he has received — that — from

pastoribus — bovem — emeret, — qui — lunae — signum — in
herdsmen — a bull — he would buy — which — of the moon — the sign — in / in / at

latere — haberet, — eumque — ante — se — ageret. — Ubi
its side / flank — would have — and it — before — himself — would act / drive — Where

decubuisset, — ibi — fatum — esse — eum — oppidum — condere
it would have laid down — there — (his) fate — to be / it was — him — a town — to build

et — ibi — regnare.
and — there — to reign

HARMODIUS ET ARISTOGITON
Harmodius — and — Aristogiton

Phalaris, — tyrannus — Akragantos — civitatis, — Harmodium
Phalaris — the tyrant / dictator — of Acragas — of the state — Harmodius

volebat — interficere, — simulationis — causa. — Scrofam
wanted — to out to death — of a feint — for the sake of — A sow

44

porcellos (piglets) habentem (having) occidit (he ~~has~~ killed) et (and) venit (he has come / came) ad (to)

Aristogitonem, (Aristogiton) amicum (friend) suum, (his) ense (with a sword {ensis5}) sanguinolento (blood-stained)

dicitque (and says) se (himself) matrem (a mother) interfecisse (to have put to death) rogatque (and asks) eum, (him) ut (that)

se (him) celaret. (he would hide) Qui (Who / And he) cum (while) ab (by) eo (him) celaretur, (was hidden) rogavit (~~has~~ asked)

Aristogitonem, (Aristogiton) ut (that) progrederetur (he would go forth) rumoresque, (and the rumours) qui (which)

essent ((there) would be) de (about) matre, (the mother) sibi (to himself) renuntiaret. (would report)

Renuntiavit (He ~~has~~ reported) nullos (not at all) esse (to be) rumores. (rumours) Qui (Who / And they) vesperi (in the evening) ita (such)

litem (a dispute {lis4}) contraxerunt, (~~have~~ contracted / entered into) ut (that) alius (the other) alio (to the other / to each other) potiora (weighty / stronger (abuse))

ingererent. (heaped upon) Aristogiton (Aristogeiton) socio (to his friend) obiecit (~~has~~ reproached) "eum (him/that he

matrem ((his, a) mother) interfecisse". (to have killed / had killed)

Deinde (Thereupon) illo (to him) Harmodius (Harmodius) patefecit (~~has~~ revealed) se ((that) he) scrofam (a sow)

porcellos (piglets) habentem (having) interfecisse (to have killed / had killed) et (and) ideo (therefore) "matrem" ("mother")

dixisse. (to have said / had said) Eo (By that) indicat (he indicates) se ((that) the) regem (the king) velle (to want / wanted) interficere (to kill)

45

rogatque eum, ut sibi adiutorio esset. Qui cum ad
and he asks him that to him as a help would be Who when at
And they

regem interficiendum venissent, deprehensi sunt a
the king in order to kill has come seized are by

satellitibus armati, et cum perducerentur ad tyrannum,
guards armed and when they were led to to the tyrant

Aristogiton a satellitibus effugit, Harmodius autem
Aristogiton from the guards ~~has~~ escaped Harmodius however

solus perductus est ad regem. Cum quaeritur ab eo,
alone conducted is to the king When he was asked by him
has been

quis ei fuisset comes, ille, ne amicum
who to him had been comrade that one that not the friend
his associate he

proderet, linguam dentibus sibi praecidit
he would betray (his) tongue with (his) teeth to himself ~~has~~ cut off

eamque regis in faciem inspuit.
and her of the king into the face ~~has~~ spit

IO
Io

Ex Inacho et Argia Io. Hanc Iuppiter dilectam
From Inachus and Argia Io (was born) That one Iupiter loved
Her

compressit et in vaccae figuram convertit, ne
~~has~~ pressed and into of a cow the shape has transformed that not
assaulted

Iuno eam cognosceret. Id Iuno cum rescivit, Argum,
Iuno her would know This Iuno when she has come Argus
came to know

cui | undique | oculi | refulgebant, | custodem | ei
at whom | all over (his body) | eyes | shone | (as a) guardian | to her

misit. | Hunc | Mercurius | Iovis | iussu | interfecit. | At
she sent | That one / Him | Mercurius | of Iupiter | on the order of | has killed | But

Iuno | formidinem | ei | misit, | cuius | timore | exagitatam
Iuno | a dread | on her | sent | of which | by the fear | disturbed

coegit | eam, | ut | se | in | mare | praecipitaret,
she has compelled | her | that | she herself | into | trhe sea | precipitated

quod | mare | Ionium | est | appellatum. | Inde | in | Scythiam
which | Sea | the Ionian | is | named | From there | to | Scythia

tranavit, | unde | Bosporum | fines | sunt
she has crossed swimming | from where | Bosporus | (those) borders region | are

dictae. | Inde | in | Aegyptum, | ubi | parit
said named | From there | to | Egypt | where | she gave birth to

Epaphum. | Iovis | cum | sciret | suapte | propter | opera
Epaphus | Iupiter | when | he knew | his own | because of | works doings

tot | eam | aerumnas | tulisse, | formam | suam | ei
so many | to her | hardships | to have borne | shape | her | to her

propriam | restituit | deamque | Aegyptiorum | eam | fecit,
own | has restored | and a goddess | of the Egyptians | her | has made

quae | Isis | nuncupatur.
who | Isis | is called by the name

MARSYAS
Marsyas

Minerva **tibias** dicitur prima ex osse cervino
Minerva / the flute / is said / first / from / a bone / of a deer

fecisse et ad epulum deorum cantatum
to have made / and / to / the banquet / of the gods / in order to sing play (it)

venisse. Iuno et Venus eam irridebant, quod et
to have come / Iuno / and / Venus / her / they derided / because / and both

caesia erat et buccas inflaret. Foeda visa et in
bluish / she was / and / cheeks / made swell / foul / seen looking / and / in

cantu irrisa in Idam silvam ad fontem venit.
her playing / derided / in to / Ida / the forest / to / a fountain / she has come came

Ibi cantans in aqua se aspexit et vidit
There / playing / in / the water / herself / she ~~has~~ watched / and / has seen saw

se merito irrisam, unde tibias ibi
(that) she / deservedly / had been derided / whence / the flute / there

abiecit et imprecata est, ut, quisquis eas
she has thrown threw away / and / pronouced a curse / is has / that / whoever / them it

sustulisset, gravi afficeretur supplicio.
would have taken take (it) up / with a heavy/severe / would be afflicted / punishment

Eas Marsyas, Oeagri filius, pastor unus e
Them It / Marsyas / of Oeagrus / son / a herdsman / one / out of

satyris invenit, quibus assidue commeletando sonum
the Satyrs / ~~has~~ found / (and) with it / regularly / by practising / a sound

suaviorem in dies faciebat, adeo ut Apollinem ad
sweeter / in day from day to day / made / so much / that / Apollo / to

citharae cantum in certamen provocaret. Quo ut
the zither / song play / in / competition / he challenged / For which / when

48

Apollo venit, Musas iudices sumpserunt, et cum
Apollo had come the Muses as judges they have taken / took and when

iam Marsyas inde victor discederet, Apollo
already Marsyas from that as victor should come out Apollo

citharam versabat idemque sonus erat; quod Marsya
the zither turned round and the same the sound was what Marsyas

tibiis facere non potuit. Itaque Apollo victum
with the flute to do not has been / was able Therefore Apollo the defeated

Marsyan ad arborem religatum Scythae tradidit,
Marsyas at / to a tree bound to a Scythian woman delivered

qui cutem ei membratim separavit. Reliquum corpus
who the skin to him limb by limb separated / stripped The remaining body

discipulo Olympo sepulturae tradidit. Ex illius
to (his) disciple Olympus for burial he ~~has~~ handed over From his

sanguine flumen Marsyas est appellatum.
blood the river Marsyas is / has been named / taken its name

MELEAGER
Meleager

Althaea, Thestii filia, ex Oeneo peperit
Althaea of Thestius daughter from Oeneus gave birth to

Meleagrum. Ibi in regia dicitur titio
Meleager There in the palace (it) is said a piece of burning wood

ardens apparuisse. Huc Parcae venerunt et
glowing to have appeared Thereupon the Parces have come / came and

49

Meliagro fata cecinerunt, eum tamdiu victurum
for Meleager (his) fate `have recited him as long wasto live
{from "cano"} that he

quamdiu is titio esset incolumis. Hinc
as -long as- that piece of wood would be unharmed Hereupon

Althaea eam titionem statim ex igne eripit et in
Althaea that piece at once out of the fire snatched and in

arca clausa diligenter servavit.
a box having been closed carefully conserved

Interim ira Dianae, quia Oeneus
In the meantime the wrath of Diana because Oeneus

sacra annua ei non fecerat, aprum
the sacred (celebrations) yearly for her not had done a boar
held

mira magnitudine qui agrum Calydonium
marvelous of size has sent which the field(s)
that he

vastaret, misit, quem Meleager cum
of the Calydonians would lay waste which Meleager together with

dilectis iuvenibus Graeciae interfecit pellemque eius
selected young men of Greece killed and hide its

ob virtute Atalantae virgini donavit, quam
because of (her) prowess to Atalanta the virgin has presented which

Althaeae fratres eripere voluerunt. Illa cum Meleagri
Althaea's brothers to snatch away have wanted She when of Meleager

fidem implorasset, ille intervenit et amorem
the faith had implored he has intervened and love
loyalty

cognationi anteposuit, avunculosque suos occidit.
blood relationship has placed before and uncles his own has killed

50

Id Althea mater ut audivit filium suum tantum
This Althea (his) mother when ~~has~~ heard son her so great

facinus esse ausum, memor Parcarum
a cdrime to be dared (to commit) remembering of the Parces
have

praecepti titionem ex arca prolatum in
-of -the instruction the block of wood from the box having brought forth into

ignem coniecit. Ita dum fratrum
the fire (it) threw In this way while (for the death) of (her) brothers

poenas vult exequi filium interfecit. At
penalty she wants to carry out (her) son she puts do death But
{poena4pl}

sorores eius praeter Gorgen et Deianiram
sisters his with the exception of Gorge ànd Deianira

flendo deorum voluntate in aves sunt transfiguratae,
weeping of the gods by the will into birds are transformed

quae "meleagridae" vocantur. At coniunx eius Alcyone
which "meleagridae" are called And spouse his Alcyone
guinea fowls

moerens in luctu decessit.
mourning in sorrow ~~has~~ passed away

REX MIDAS
King Midas

Midas rex Mygdonius filius Matris deae a Timolo
Midas king the Mygdonian son of Mater the goddess by Timolus
Cybele

arbiter sumptus eo tempore, quo Apollo cum
as arbiter has been taken in that time in which Apollo with
when

Marsya | vel | Pane | fistula | certavit. | Quod | cum | Timolus
Marsyas | or | Pan | on the flute | competed | Because | when | Timolus

victoriam | Apollini | daret, | Midas | dixit | Marsyae | potius
the triumph | to Apollo | gave | Midas | has said | to Marsyas | rather

dandam. | Tunc | Apollo | indignatus | Midae | dixit: | "Quale
should be given | then | Apollo | indignant | to Midas | has said | Such as

cor | in | iudicando | habuisti, | tales | et | auriculas
a heart | in | judging | you have had | such | also | ears

habebis." | Quibus | auditis | effecit, | ut
you will have | This | having heard | he has made/brought about | that
| | ablativus absolutus | |

asininas | haberet | aures.
as a donkey | he would have | ears

Eo | tempore | Liber | pater | cum | exercitum | in | Indiam
At that | time | Liber | the Father | when | (his) army | to | India
| {tempus5} | Bacchus | | | swarm | |

duceret | Silenus | aberravit, | quem | Midas | hospitio
led | Silenus | has wandered off | whom | Midas | as a guest
| | | and him | |

liberaliter | accepit | atque | ducem | dedit, | qui | eum | in
liberally | received | and | a guide | has given | who | him | to
| | | | gave | | |

comitatum | Liberi | deduceret. | At | Midae | Liber | pater
the company | of Liber | should lead back | And | to Midas | Liber | Father

ob | beneficium | deoptandi | dedit | potestatem, | ut,
because of | (that) good deed | to choose | has given | the power | that
| | | gave | |

quicquid | vellet, | peteret | a | se. | A | quo | Midas
whatever | he would like | he would ask | from | him | From | whom | Midas

petiit, | ut, | quicquid | tetigisset, | aurum | fieret.
has asked | that | whatever | he would have touched | gold | would become

52

Quod **cum** **impetrasset** **et** **in** **regiam** **venisset,**
What / That — when — he had obtained — and — into — the palace — he had come

quicquid **tetigerat,** **aurum** **fiebat.** **Cum** **iam** **fame**
whatever — he had touched — gold — became — When — already — by hunger

cruciaretur, **petit** **a** **Libero,** **ut** **sibi** **speciosum**
he was tortured — he asked — from — Liber — that — from him — the specious

donum **eriperet;** **quem** **Liber** **iussit** **in** **flumine**
present — would take away — him / and him — Liber — has ordered — in — the river

Pactolo **se** **abluere.** **Cuius** **corpus** **aquam** **cum**
Pactolus — himself — to bathe — Whose / And his — body — the water — when

tetigisset, **facta** **est** **colore** **aureo;** **quod** **flumen** **nunc**
had touched — become — it is / has — of a color — golden — which — river — now

Chrysorrhoas **appellatur** **in** **Lydia.**
Chrysorrhoas / Goldstream — is named — in — Lydia

NIOBE
Niobe

Amphion **et** **Zetus** **Iovis** **et** **Antiopes** **Nyctei** **filii**
Ampjion — and — Zetus — of Iupiter — and — Antiope — of Nycteus — daughter

iussu **Apollinis** **Thebas** **muro** **circumcinxerunt** **usque**
by order — of Apollo — Thebes — with a wall — have surrounded — until

ad **Semelae** **bustum.** **Laium** **Labdaci** **regis** **filium** **in**
at — of Semele — the mound — Laius — of Labdacus — king {rex2} — the son — in

exsilium **eiecerunt,** **ipsi** **ibi** **regnum** **obtinere**
exile — they have sent away — themselves — there — the kingdom — to obtain

coeperunt. (have begun) **Amphion** (Amphion) **rex** (king) **in** (in) **coniugium** (marriage) **Niobam,** (Niobe) **Tantali** (of Tantalus)

et (and) **Diones** (Dione) **filiam,** (daughter) **accepit.** (has received) **Ex** (From) **ea** (her) **procreavit** (he has begotten / begot) **liberos** (children / sons)

septem (seven) **totidemque** (and as many) **filias.** (daughters)

Eum (This) **partum** (birth / offspring) **Niobe** (Niobe) **Latonae** (Latona) **deae** (the goddess) **anteposuit** (valued above)

superbiusque (and haughtyly) **locuta** (spoken) **est** (she is / has) **in** (to) **Apollinem** (Apollo) **et** (and) **Dianam,** (Diana)

quod (because) **illa** (she (Diana)) **cincta** (girded/dressed) **viri** (of a man) **cultu** (with clothes) **esset** (would be / was) **et** (and)

Apollo (Apollo) **veste** (with dress dressed) **deorsum** (downwards) **atque** (and) **crinitus,** (long-haired) **et** (and) **se** (she herself)

numero (in number) **filiorum** (of children) **Latonam** (Latona) **superare.** (surpassed) **Ob** (Because of) **id** (this) **Apollo** (Apollo)

filios (sons) **eius** (her) **in** (in) **silva** (a forest) **venantes** (hunting) **sagittis** (with arrows) **interfecit** (has killed) **et** (and)

Diana (Diana) **filias** (the daughters) **in** (in) **regia** (the palace) **sagittis** (with arrows) **interemit** (has slain / slew) **praeter** (except for)

Chloridem. (Chloris) **At** (And) **genetrix** (the mother) **liberis** (of children) **orba** (bereft) **flendo** (by weeping) **lapidea** (of stone)

facta (made / become) **esse** (to be) **dicitur** (is said) **in** (on) **monte** (Mount) **Sipylo,** (Sipylus) **eiusque** (and of her) **hodie** (daily)

lacrimae (tears) **manare** (to flow) **dicuntur.** (are said) **Amphion** (Amphion) **autem** (however) **cum** (when) **templum** (the temple)

Apollinis   expugnare   vellet,   ab   Apolline   sagittis   est
of Apollo   to assault   he wanted   by   Apollo   with arrows   is

interfectus.
killed

TANTALUS
Tantalus

Tantalus,   Iovis   et   Plutonis   filius,   procreavit   ex   Dione
Tantalus   of Iupiter   and   Pluto   son   generated   from   Dione

Pelopem.   Iuppiter   Tantalo   concredere   sua   consilia   solitus
Pelops   Iupiter   to Tantalus   to confide   his   counsels   used

erat   et   ad   epulum   deorum   admittere,   quae
was   and   at   the banquet   of the gods   (him) to admit   which (counsels)

Tantalus   ad   homines   renuntiavit;   ob   id   dicitur
Tantalus   to   the people   reported   Because of   that   he is said

ad   inferos   in   aqua   media   fine   corporis   stare
to the   underworld   in   water   middle   limit   of (his) body   to stand
        up to his waist

semperque   sitire   et,   cum   haustum   aquae   vult
and always   to be thirsty   and   when   a draught   of water   he wants

sumere,   aquam   recedere.   Item   poma   ei   super
to take   the water   to recede   Likewise   fruits   him   over
  that the water recedes

caput   pendent,   quae   cum   vult   sumere,   rami
(his) head   hang   which   when   he wants   to take   the branches
    and these

vento   moti   recedunt.   Item   saxum   super   caput   eius
by the wind   moved   recede   Likewise   a stone   over   head   his

ingens pendet, quod semper timet ne super se
very big hangs which always `he fears that not upon himself

ruat.
crashes down

TIRESIAS
Tiresias

In monte Cyllenio Tiresias, Eueris filius, pastor,
In Mount Cyllene Tiresias of Euerius son herdsman
On

dracones venerantes dicitur baculo percussisse, alias
snakes mating is said with (his) staff to have struck others

calcasse. Ob id in mulieris figuram est
to have trampled upon Because of this into of a woman the shape he is

conversus. Postea monitus a sortibus in eodem
transformed Afterwards advised by oracle sayings in the same

loco dracones cum calcasset, redit in
place the snakes (as) when he had trampled upon he has come back into

pristinam speciem.
former (his) shape

Eodem tempore inter Iovem et Iunonem fuit
At the same time between Iupiter and Iuno (there) has been

iocosa altercatio, quis magis de re venerea
playful argument who more from thing of love
sex

voluptatem caperet, masculus an femina. De qua re
pleasure would take the male or the female On which thing
question

56

Tiresiam **iudicem** **sumpserunt,** **qui** **utrunque** **erat**
Tiresias — as judge — they have taken took — who — both — was/had

expertus. **Is** **cum** **secundum** **Iovem** **iudicasset,** **Iuno**
expercienced — He — when — in accordance with — Iupiter — had judged — Iuno

irata **manu** **aversa** **eum** **excaecavit.** **At** **Iovis** **ob**
angered — with (her) — back — him — ~~has~~ blinded — But — Iupiter — because of

id **fecit,** **ut** **septem** **aetates** **viveret** **vatesque**
that — ~~has~~ made — that — seven — ages — he would live — and a diviner

praeter **ceteros** **mortales** **esset.**
above — the other — mortals — would be